THE STORY OF NO

Emma Hammond' first collection, *tunth-sk*, was published in 2011 by Flipped Eye. In addition she has self-published two pamphlets, *softly softly catchy monkey* and *Sleeveless Errand*. She has performed at many events in London over the last ten years. Emma works as a freelance copywriter and has taught experimental poetry for the Poetry School. In her spare time she mentors children at the Ministry of Stories.

PRAISE FOR EMMA HAMMOND

'There is something about the imaginative control exercised by Hammond, coupled with metaphorical daring, that makes you read on. The poetry is wild and unsettling but also cool and convincingly modern. This is the poetry of lived experience, but also of lived writing. Though seemingly utterly spontaneous it is also very self-aware. As if it is the most natural thing in the world, she manages to capture the life of the mind, even as it captures the movements of the world. Surprise is the engine of a good poem and Emma Hammond never fails to provide this element. She is the real thing.'
      Hugo Williams

ALSO BY EMMA HAMMOND

POETRY

tunth-sk (Flipped Eye Publishing, 2011)

The Story of No
Emma Hammond

Penned in the Margins
LONDON

PUBLISHED BY PENNED IN THE MARGINS
Toynbee Studios, 28 Commercial Street, London E1 6AB
www.pennedinthemargins.co.uk

All rights reserved
© Emma Hammond 2015

The right of Emma Hammond to be identified as the author of this work has been asserted by her in accordance with Section 77 of the Copyright, Designs and Patent Act 1988.

This book is in copyright. Subject to statutory exception and to provisions of relevant collective licensing agreements, no reproduction of any part may take place without the written permission of Penned in the Margins.

First published 2015

Printed in the United Kingdom by TJ International.

ISBN
978-1-908058-30-0

This book is sold subject to the condition that it shall not, by way of trade or otherwise, be lent, re-sold, hired out, or otherwise circulated without the publisher's prior consent in any form of binding or cover other than that in which it is published and without a similar condition including this condition being imposed on the subsequent purchaser.

CONTENTS

Space	11
Status	13
Death	15
Lemonade	17
Auk	19
Unit	20
Utility	21
Lego	23
Hairdresser	24
Catsuit	26
Trinity	28
Eggs	30
Thinkpiece	35
Tax	36
End	37
Realpolitik	38
Milk	39
Pine	41
Interchange	43
Bored	45
Creed	47
Equality	49
Mini-break	51
Fire	53

Expert	56
Order	57
Cremation	59
Crumpet	61
Troubadour	63

THANKS

Thanks to Dan and Flo.

For Mum

The Story of No

Space

The view across the table leads not to the sea
as the multi-spiked flowers might suggest

but rather towards a piecemeal idea of future life
called 'I have done it and have a dog called SNIP.'

He is a good dog but Boy does he blend
and run all over chasing a tale or 2
to tell at glitzy parties in his best ruffle.

Well, I'm not sure I have time for that kind of thing;
I have other people's art to look at
and it takes up *a lot of time*. I barely

do anything else and my fingers are worn to the
bone — I have blisters from gripping the days in a
semblance of doing... it's exhausting Son.

While all through this the drought makes mirages
in the shape of space, I shuffle towards them but
like an eyeless magpie miss the glint. Oh my

it's probably better to be enrolled, yet the grass
is dead. My therapist has broke her foot and I want
to put her in a litter. I will ask her if this is normal

with my common sense face, and she will say
But what happens when we reach the sea?
in a voice of wonder, of dread.

Status

Sorley Pinkles has lost his dog. The
profile is not looking good. Half his head
is missing, you must adjust. Loads of likes —
over a *dog*... what? My dead

Granny got less than that. Pert in black
& white, her mystery all cached up. Not good
enough. Hashtag awful isn't it. Nobody
cares. Augustus Caravel uploads

sixteen images. Let's have a look then.
Sunset, paella, hotdog legs, gaping wound —
WAIT, what? Waterski, water*melon*, water,
blank face, so humour!

PegLeg Loonbucket has tagged me in 5 new
pictures. In 3 I'm the moon, but in others
I am reclining on a chaise longue with a glass
flower in my vagina. I look amazing.

I look amazing, I type in the box. *What a night!*
PegLeg likes my comment. *I know,* he writes.

Looking good hun xxxxx. I flick to his page
and mindlessly browse through 278 profile pics.

He's so cool I think. *What an original.* Sorley is
worrying about the dog by posting filtered snaps
in X-pro and that new one, Arctic Storm.
In any case it makes Cracker look arty and wild.

Where did you last see Cracker? I type, but I'm
not sure I care too much tbh. Cracker always
had too much exposure. No wonder he's been nicked,
battered to death, stuffed in a wheelie bin.

Death

Gulfs appear around the
crockery. Laura Ashley
is a type of Death. Death by
Thank you notes. Death

by balled socks. Cath Kitson is
a type of illness. Cupcakes are a
coven of witches. Sex is messy.
Seven more sleeps. Weddings:

a type of sleep. You are invited
to the Earth's core. *Pass
the eyeless worm.* Death is averted
through children. Ovulate.

Close your legs. Love! Nigella
is a goddess. Knit your own
manchild. Disapprove. Bake yourself
into a pie of birds. Death

is invisible. It's all
about the dress. Skip the bread.

Match the cagoules. Decorate the baby.
Pry open the magazine. Death

in the washing machine. Death
in the bath bomb. A waterfall of blood
at the school gates. Guard the nucleus.
Ward off demons. Cry

in the dark. Where is your husband?
Where is ze family? Grieve for your pelvic floor.
Infiltrate the Relaxing Spa for Me Time.
Gasp –

Lemonade

The Russian handyman found a grot mag
under my bed. The headboard is loose; you need
lemonade in the floor. Lemonade? Who even

reads pornos anymore? It's not the eighties!
I went to a cafe to escape but the woman said
Are you all right? in a way that made me think my

mouth might be doing that criss-cross thing, like in
Anthropology when the teacher said
You look confused, what is it? — my resting face

sort of awful. And my landlord with the spiffy
clothes says he is disappointed in me and wants
to deconstruct our relationship but I can't take it

seriously. Fungus
lingers under the floor. I am ejected into
the winter. Laminate! Well, we could all do with

a bit of that. My breath exits my mouth and I am
aimless, hobbling up a hill on ball bearings.

Time to change my paradigm says the tick-tock —

I'm not fucking Sylvia Plath! Too much of a pussy
to put my head anywhere near an oven. Nothing.
Sergej found a rat's bed. Remember that time you

woke up with your trousers down?
Yeah, well every girl does — you're not special.

Auk

Little Auk of the green corridors,
Arctic flip-flap of the undug dugout,
alluvium piper of wetted socks

and the great spines of tyres —
sit you on Treacle Mustard,
the untiled roof of this

brokedown house,
the business eyes that coat you in flint;
Sing to them of knick-knacks,

this spear-head, done-in lake
meandered to death in wandering,
O Little Auk!

Flit you across the axe-rich earth,
so bright high over the red hoods
of the two-wheeled men.

Unit

Lucy Harvest, our lady of the abandoned beaches

Amy, extreme godmother of key cherry orchards

Amy 2, wild swims in the maths of lichen

Jesse: won't stop

Barbara — businessman. Strong of auburn glory-hole

Holly and the river of Spall. Bloody knight's sword, cut

One day we'll

Utility

Mum is dying of cancer. She exists in a box. It is cold there in the utility room. A bright pink piece of salmon slides from the fridge onto her hand. Do you want it? she says. Let me give it to you. It has a month in it, but the expiry date is today. I don't understand and I feel bad that I don't want the fish. I don't want it, or the trousers — they are a *good make*. I don't want the trousers or the soap. Everyone gave her soap for Christmas because it runs out.

I got her poems about the war. She talks about the snowdrops and those little yellow ones. Ma is an artist really, painter of storms. She speaks of gusto and billy-o, things *blow a hooley*. She flattens her *y*s to *ee*s. Recently she sits under a blanket and looks out across the garden watching the birds behind the glazing. You can sell the silver on eBay, she says. I don't want the fucking silver but it is a *loose end*.

Your sister has earmarked the Chinese paintings. What do you want? I close her fragile body in a hug. We are boisterous in talk of corpse preparation. I've done it more times than you've had hot dinners, she says. You stuff them with cotton wool and tie their necks back. She weaves an invisible knot and yanks it tight. Words push their way out of us like fingers pointing toward nothing, hard to know where to.

And her dead friend imported coffins from China. They took so long to get here that the bamboo started sprouting so were useless! We laugh about that and how he was the *life and soul*. She tucks her little feet into slippers. The worst thing is that I love you all so much she says with a little blip. The clocks soon go. Remember how she used to make us dance a *Céilí* in the wilderness? The fury running through her like sense.

Lego

What we really need is a new sculpture made of Lego.
Mr. Featherstonehaugh the *social* artist is working on
a huge pair of testicles to symbolise the rise of Mansplaining
in a post-post-feminist world. Here is the privilege, just next to
the Spermatic cord. Primrose Hill will carry the plastic,
multi-coloured testes as a kind of radical Angel of the North.

I close the tab and stare off into the distance. *Am I even real?*
I say to the cat, but the cat died 4 months ago and does not
know. I wonder what is happening on the *Daily Mail?* It is a
woman from that show about a show that is on TV but also not
at the same time. She has enormous breasts in Dubai. My
stomach is an earthquake, the tectonic plates all shifted up.

Magenta is the new turquoise. I am genuinely surprised but it
doesn't last. Take This Quiz To Find Out If You've Lost The
Will To Live. I have a) Lost the will to live. My tweet about how
Twitter is the last refuge of the lost soul gets RTed by a semi-
famous clown troupe, The Lost Souls of Didcot Parkway.
Things are definitely looking up! The rain types hard on the
                                                            window.

Hairdresser

instagram sounds ok she say.
yes i went there once or twice in my youth i say,
it is a bit like the 80s when groups of friends were still american.
oh ya she say and looks at herself over my hair —
i remember that — i went to see bands that weren't famous.
yeah, me too! i say. *in the 90s it was the same.*
remember t-shirts with pen on? and lockjaw? we laugh.
yeah we were crazy back then. i stare at my face.
nowadays though of course i am a grown up, it means some things.
oh yeah for sure she say.
*nowadays i have different outlooks, with alternating colours in them —
death is close. maybe i will have a staycation instead on twitter.*
it is colder there but with content.
nah she say, *twitter is kinda dirty.*

i stare out the window and see a small dog
in a hand-knitted jumper. the old crafts are back in.
my hair is coming on, it is in a shape.
my boyfriend is at war again she says —
he is asleep. she corrects her posture.
ages ago he was a hunter-gatherer.
yeah i say, *i know what you mean.*

Emma Hammond

a song comes on, it say *do it do it do it, shake!*
i love this one she say and moves her hips. an old lady
is authentic in the corner.

seen any films lately? say the man slightly to the left.
oh ya say my one,
it was about how we're all the same and do the same things.
great! say he. *you're not married are you?*
he looks at me all vicious.
no i say, *i am married to myself!* laughter.
at least you won't ever leave yourself! he say.
no i say, *i will never forget my own anniversary!*
it doesn't quite make sense but everyone laughs.
it is quiet then apart from
do it do it do it shake! and all suddenly awkward.

the old lady takes out a handkerchief like a prop and blows out her
ancient insides.
the problem with you youngsters she say *is that you get bored of things
too easily.*
it is a pretty boring thing to say.
i can't even finish an article i say, *let alone a life!*
this time nobody laughs — it really doesn't make any sense.

Catsuit

7 and encased in the velvet catsuit purple with the white piping,
on the edge of a bridge where water slipped past like a ghostling

was I — with my little feet dangling and the roaring in my reddened
                              ears saying
SATURDAY as Dad was one-hand pushing the clouds out and Mum

was home with John Player and her radio and basting things
like a cricket rubbing her legs together and crying or whatever.

so here we were on Timmy's Lane where lovers came,
this Essex Shangri-La where I would give boys great head™ later on

and I was staring into the water which rushed under me and
through the pooh stick tunnel but all I knew was *I hate this catsuit in*
                              the shape of me

so I put myself further on the rim and tipped my body off until I was
                              falling for
miles and miles upside down like a Red Arrow with smoke which
                              wrote

O God and my face hit the water and the waves came inside the
                              suit and blew
me up and I heard Dad say *Ho!* and he jumped in the river and
                              grabbed me

with a hand the size of that kid's house whose dad was put in prison
                              and I was
saved not dead and the smoke from the spinney spilled into tears and

cried me all the way home in my cocoon of skin down Crow Lane
where the crows made nests and swooped me up in caws when the sun
                              came up

and onward still to Goblin Hill where I was made — over the sewer and
                              lost plastic
men the graves of cats and all the nooks out back where the chickens
                              screamed.

Trinity

The baby peers out of the screen
like Stay Puft in a babygro with stags
it pushes a hand-crafted 3 wheeled wooden
stroller called Fantasy with zoomed in
eyes so large they lurch out at me like wolves
in woods *v pink* and mostly your
terrible hands like starfish wave out into
the darkest night with breast milk for making

Your Husband and Furniture and
Family the chin (his) with no shouting no
schism *you freeze* Baby Food and talk about
Schedules and Sophie le giraffe is day-glo
so appropriate with stages and well defined
Grandparents who come and visit your
nest with Casseroles and Hammers
and how Porky Pig is growing up

In fancy wallpapers and no slugs beginning
words like Bumbo and Upholstery and
Carry on Dad in smiling pictures of the
3 of you and life is an album of Yes

and hand prints in plaster and marks on walls
going up & up in the Feed and high
up always into the middle of the night
where you grip yourself in some inimitable No

Eggs

* 1885 Hen
* 1886 Hen with Sapphire Pendant†
* 1887 Blue Serpent Clock
* 1888 Cherub with Chariot†
* 1889 Nécessaire†
* 1890 Danish Palaces
* 1891 Memory of Azov
* 1892 Diamond Trellis
* 1893 Caucasus
* 1894 Renaissance
* 1895 Rosebud
* 1895 Twelve Monograms
* 1896 Revolving Miniatures
* 1896 Alexander III Portraits†
* 1897 Coronation
* 1897 Mauve†
* 1898 Lilies-of-the-Valley
* 1898 Pelican

* 1899 Bouquet of Lilies Clock
* 1899 Pansy
* 1900 Trans-Siberian Railway

* 1900 Cockerel
* 1901 Basket of Wild Flowers
* 1901 Gatchina Palace
* 1902 Clover Leaf
* 1902 Empire Nephrite†
* 1903 Peter the Great
* 1903 Royal Danish†
* 1904 No eggs made
* 1905 No eggs made
* 1906 Moscow Kremlin
* 1906 Swan
* 1907 Rose Trellis
* 1907 Cradle with Garlands
* 1908 Alexander Palace
* 1908 Peacock

* 1909 Standart Yacht
* 1909 Alexander III Commemorative†
* 1910 Colonnade
* 1910 Alexander III Equestrian
* 1911 Fifteenth Anniversary
* 1911 Bay Tree
* 1912 Czarevich
* 1912 Napoleonic
* 1913 Romanov Tercentenary
* 1913 Winter

* 1914 Mosaic
* 1914 Grisaille
* 1915 Red Cross with Triptych
* 1915 Red Cross with Imperial Portraits
* 1916 Steel Military
* 1916 Order of St. George
* 1917 Karelian Birch
* 1917 Constellation (unfinished)

* 1898 Hen
* 1899 Twelve Panel
* 1900 Pine Cone
* 1901 Apple Blossom
* 1902 Rocaille
* 1903 Bonbonnière
* 1904 Chanticleer

* 1885-1891 Blue Striped Enamel
* 1902 Duchess of Marlborough
* 1902 Rothschild
* 1907 Youssoupov
* 1914 Nobel Ice
* 1885-1889 Resurrection
* 1899-1903 Spring Flowers

† Indicates missing egg

East

Whatsit hits the cymbal
while bearded men with tackle
clap ecstatically.

Private jokes fall on woodblocks.
A woman in white moves
silently down the aisle, her hand

clasped around a clef. Leisure
for the urban entity
here in the disused railway arch,

the haircut gallery. Black
oversized poetry about LOLcats.
A poem in an evaporating dish

As Genie. The poem as object
or electric Jew. Disassembled
hardcore in trainers,

Consumption. As beer made from
the tongues of metropolitan bees.

Ironic dancing in the style of

Non-ironic dancing. Clever
commentary on Twitter vs
clever commentary about

The commentary on Twitter. Poems
about the commentary vs the clever
commentary. Secret

Goosebumps to Coldplay. Online
irreverence and complex bravado.
This, our collective hurt.

Thinkpiece

Renee Zellweger's face has changed
We hate Renee Zellweger's new face
Ten reasons why we all hate Renee Zellweger's new face
Renee Zellweger's face has not changed, it is we who have changed
We need to change the way we think about Renee Zellweger's face
The world we live in has changed Renee Zellweger's face
We love Renee Zellweger's new face
Ten reasons why we all love Renee Zellweger's new face
We should all change our faces like Renee Zellweger
Why should Renee Zellweger have to talk about her face?
Renee Zellweger should be talking about her face
Will Renee Zellweger's new face win an Oscar?
We must not notice that Renee Zellweger's face changed.
Stop noticing
If you noticed that Renee Zellweger's face changed,
you are a bad person
The world is changing, it's not just Renee Zellweger's face
Change is inevitable

Tax

What about these Dinner Lady positions?
say Job Thing, her face all atoms. The poster
behind her shows a Magical Negro learning New
Skills. *You must use a teaspoon to empty out the
River Thames into the mouths of Lost Children.*
Her lips go Interrobang. Should've had an abortion —
gin / coat hanger then straight back to your desk
on Mundee. *Looking for a Job: a Job in itself.*
Hardworking Taxpayer spins sad on a pivot —

clean out of Meal Deals. Particle Lady
spells out Workfare by rolling a boulder slowly
up and down my arm. She is punctured
skin in pools on the Job Centre floor, soft
money that trickles to my useless hands. My feet
stuck fast in molten fury — *How will I get back
to my Luxury Lifestyle now? I chose wrong!*
My arm rises and plunges a Biro into my own chest.
The adventure ends here.

End

My cat is dead. His little vein wouldn't take the needle. He is under the ground in the back garden turning to liquid. I taped up the cat flap with packing tape. I dream of him and enlarge pictures of his eyes. I don't know where he went. Soon my Mum will die and I'll probably feel guilty because I never phone her. Her limbs are thin as twigs from the cancer. She will fold up in the earth like a collapsed clothes dryer.

I do the school run then say hello to the man in the Viking shop and the little man from the mini mart. They exist in my life. I can't, I don't know where they go. Trying to read *Moby Dick* but the words keep skipping about. I think I have anger issues. Boring. Trying not to dress like a Mum when you are a Mum. A choice of shoe. A dream about an eight-year-old calling you a pig. The tree is up in the square. I don't. The nights are so. And everyone married, like defeat.

Realpolitik

Oh yes, **she tuts.** *It is quite an awful reality. I haven't voted since 1971 and that was just to impress that Derek. He beat me in the end and left me in a pool of toenail cuttings, singing Mariah Carey.*

Milk

A rolling hitch, eye splice
and under the skin-fur
a noose, there. If I bread you
out like ginger then
cut you here and there
you might be tiny men or
snaps.

My hand is a nest of cramp,
skinny-jean fingers,
shrunk-fit. I pummel you
slight as bird-hopped snow
in the yolky sun.

Here, I love you. My beak
of twigs, iced gems —
morninghasbroken mice
twisted cherry stalks, a dagger
of mirror, springs
in your thorax gone
ah ha,

I love you. I cannot put my
hand into you. Cat-gut strung
knuckled in bunches of words,
we appear and leave, top-most
of trees and breeze. A comet
burns through us — in a while
the darkness, bright as an organ
follows.

My saucer of milk. Far away
you send me pieces of violence —
a boy-shaped mouth in my fabric
and your Lucian Gregory blood
spilled out nice in the road.

Pine

Hurts the room with her hands, with boxes of *nope*
wrapped in pictures of woodlands, one with that stag
caught mid-run or -hunt, his terrified eye turned bright
to church with its cold fingers and bows. *What*

did you get in your stocking? says dog man. I sing
Polly put the kettle on, even though Polly is a doll
and I know her cloth hands would burn up and
tea would just go down her face

like gin! Tinsel thin as a girl, Rosalie & Malcolm's
is full of smoke and Wotsits, a seaside postcard of
rotten lungs. *All right love?* say the Dads. *All right
Malc* I said, or Jim or Andy — my velvet dress turned red

& back to chopping. Terrible pile-ups of veg, little crosses
on the sprouts and icicle parsnips snipped to bits, gravy in a boat
that sails across the kitchen in brown shanties, pudding
that comes in with blue fire, vivid as a ghost.

Dad snaps off the Queen's speech. I open a word processor
to write poems about Auks. Mum is sad about the high-heeled

slippers. We walk down the lane and pretend
to be dragons with smoke coming out... thorn rhinos —

those snowflakes you cut with the holes.

Interchange

Beautiful girls serve coffee in shops
as orchids. Golden hair & excellent
people skills, rare faces — wondrous
tundras, goblet drums. Sugar? So

Chirpy. The woman in the Co-op's
knowing smile, I love her. And sawdust
man in the Pet Shop fires out fiery fish
to passers-by with dying eyes,

battening down hutches, tending to the
marrowbone. This, plus the kindness
of milk, the human of everyone. Scurrying
army of Scuse me. A glove on a fence

waves neon into the morning. Lost
marbles and laughter at the glass
English voices — there is no gap. Elvis
on the night bus, the flicker of ubiquity

in all things. Lunatics on street corners
and Mr Metcalfe in his mum's pink socks

filming his wonder tales, diatribes —
all-fronting to salute the beautiful How.

Bored

Not Bored. Group
holidays with OK
pavlova. A hip flask.
Quirks, the death
of West Egg.

Your wife is caught in
terrible crisis. Alert-
faced. Lined with
Faux Fur, the eyes of
a flowered teacup.

The New Enthusiasm,
occasional blow jobs
and elaborately
bloody meat: yodelling
in gingham.

Shark-toothed bunting.
Your profile pushes a ball of
dung across the responsive,
causing birds to comment

hard in breadcrumbs.

Roleplay vs Realplay,
expression: *hilarious,*
tight jaws clamped onto isms
for blunting the hinterlands
of your Cognitive Bias.

Keep Calm and Posit tho —
crack open the vintage cunt :-)
Be sure to talk about your
Working Class Roots!
Kill yourselves.

Creed

Nattering about a *voice* in hushed
Reverence. This is not a church
You tit. If I am Death then you are
The embodiment, chattering nut
Crackers dressed in English
Niceness — the most dangerous

Type. Backstage you prattle
Of psychological duress and how
Powerful you feel, keeping your
Fingers curled tight around your
Precious and wearing the exact
Right fantasies of future brilliance.

You walk around me, braying spume
And legacy, the mind of someone
Living — *Anyone could do that!* you
Bark into my black hanging mouth —
Sucking off your pen like some
Ding dong auditor, not entirely sure

If you can allow it. This world within,

This tank of hurt and pointedness.
The knowledge that there is no God
Nor self to keep, yet always
The impossibility of death, futility —
The misread despair of a shark.

Equality

Cougar helps teens with her experienced
Glamour babe fingering in panties

Latina babe Megan Salinas passionate
French amateur fucks fake taxi driver

Newbie sweetheart Myrna Joy gets
Chelsea brought a friend with

Pov fucking Mia banggg
Sexy blonde milf named Ashley

Goth babe huge black cock
Bubble butt sweetie Nomi

Slender babe teases he
Certified Latina cutie anal r

Having sex fun with my blonde GF
Cheerleader fucks her skinny BF

University Student's first sextape

Teen begs to be fucke

Blonde fucked in corset stockings
Oiled white feet fuck

Busty teen banged and cr
Teen shows her body proudly

Innocent teen takes it in the ass
Tit fucked step sis teen

Slutty teen compelled to
High heel milf blows cock

College amateurs eat out
Interracial slut fucked

Horny girl gets her ars
Every woman adores a Fasc

Mini-break

Période, and the tower out the
Window. It was transported over ze
Sea! Well that's one way, isn't-it-not.
Romance is a dead horse — Nietzsche
Knew about that. Gendarmes
Guard the girders and Hitler
Only had one boule — he held the
Key in his grubbed up mitt — a Man.

We traverse the Tuileries and look at yon
Kittiwake. He hisses and drives back the
Dross. *Get out*, he squawks and pierces the
Enemy. The golden ball that rests on the
Water is just for show — this will end
Badly. Faces in a cafe and old skins lying
Around like off a snake. Casual tears and
A church with crosses made from driftwood

Or birch. I am jealous of the peace. There
Is no peace. I think the idea brings me
Peace. Paris. And what
Are you? A beautiful pile of rubble.

The river is high with rain. Padlocks flap
In the thin wind. People try and hang onto things.
In danger of exploding — our bags are full of

Weapons. We are terrorists and terrify
Ourselves. But what about we say. *What
About?* And all these bones. What about these
Six million sets of ivories! You kiss me hard
In the bedroom and we wonder about the
Girl in the wallpaper, the rakish Gent-bird,
Hurt by exactitude —
Ossifying in the dark like a self.

Fire

1.

Autumn is sexually attractive
with its nakedness and pitfalls.
Dads like Autumn as they get to burn stuff:
men stuffed with knickers.

Scrabbling round my room in the darkness
he looks for his Club. I nicked it and marvelled
at the open women. I don't get it. He woke me up
but I threw it in a stream.

He saw me at the Barbican later. He said
*Who is this gorgeous creature who is
my daughter?* When I got fat he went off me —
I was not sexually attractive.

After the hurricane we went to his friend's.
Diana didn't smell of hospitals —
she was a red-haired forest of breasts,
ripped from the ground by a storm.

I have also been, like a soldier. Efficient
in my bubbliness, crop spraying mystery
across the stubble of Essex fields, yellow
with rape — choking on the oil-smell of beach huts.

And I have been — good as gold, named you
Wonderful, listened to your ideas while you
stare out to sea, bobbing off on the
black Clacton tide.

2.

Women, though,
are worst. With their sideways
glances and unspoken speaks,
great hags with flaps, busting

movement into weekdays. Not as posh
as that nor Olde Worlde neither.
Mothers with their thoughts and waiting.
Smoking in the out-of-date

kitchen, one slipper flipping like a
whale. PUT IT IN THE BIN she shouts,
knocking back a flaming shot from the
microwave. I'LL SAY 'FUCKING CHICKENS'

WHENEVER I FUCKING WELL LIKE.
We get tipped into the lemon meringue,
all of us, rolled around in the Hansel & Gretel
or baked en croute in our shells of bodies.

She smuggles the sanitary towels past the Men.
I'VE GOT YOUR BUNNIES she whispers,
MY MOTHER USED TO BURN THEM ON A FIRE.

Expert

My hands rest on the wood like two
small squid, ragged and cramped
from the biting. You have been
dead for exactly one week, and if
I think about it my mind will not.

Podgy in a grasp of fingers
rough as terrain from binding,
fending off ghosts on the night ward
and prank calls to enemies, you cup
my face in them, drunk on it.

You're my chicken, you say —
and I pummel your creaky feet,
the two small boats that sailed you
across the surfaces of broken
mirrors toward laughter and gin,

duets in the sun, Pookie,
SodaStream. Battleaxe — how
are you disappeared? My Magpie,
bright paradox, expert of experts,
all conjuror of love — absent Yes.

Order

Wading out, I put your life in the bin.
What is a hoarder? No oarder. Easy now!
Your X-ray specs in a black bag, wigs,
your knicker draw — pretty avant-garde.

We can dress it up. The dispensary was
your friend— like a sleeping rattlesnake, rattling
all the azepams. Out of date, I empty things.
Pills like hail into *chuck*. The other *charity*.

The jellyfish hat you wore then hated, it is
a reflected moon. All the notes from 1965 —
into the bin. There is a rat in the back room, he is
nibbling the bibles. *Bloody cheek* you'd say.

Congratulations on the birth of your baby boy —
bin it. Telegrams. Dustbin. Ten thousand
pillows, heavy with dreams. Blood. Stop.
The garden overgrown as Sleeping Beauty,

orders of service for Katherine, for James.
Weddings, brochures of escape — *recycling*,
the legend of your going away dress. I felt it

in the childhood part, the silk, the purple,

the doily-white one — screwed into a ball in a
smashy chest with the *sgian-dubh*. What a waist!
I could reach round it with my two hands, if the
insects would just *fuck off*. Your enormous eyes,

we dress them up. Twelve forever with your flashing
presents, every card squirrelled, every seashell.
A sudden picture of your Father in a pocket — so
many mints, gums. Your teeth. A lock of hair.

Auto-clean. Super-disperse. I am a cleaning
robot. All the furnishings are damp, melting.
A likeness I made of an owl, into the bin.
Bad watches, a million run out pens, *ruthless*.

The Snoopy sweatshirt, last seen in
1987. Tangles of jewellery wrapped hard around
the propellor. A lost bear, unbearable. Haha.
The tears come quietly. We can make it sound

eccentric! I open another draw knowing it will
contain years and years and years and. Finished
lipsticks, dead shoes. Your nightie still on the bed.
I clean up your face with a hanky.

Cremation

Today like a Christmas list
you are going up the chimney.
A tangerine or lump of coal, no
keys to a sports car / your logic.

The portal goes up in smoke.
Your skin a *ta dah!* vanished with
white bone magic, Raspberry
Ripple traces and metal

shot through like rivers on a map.
Where have you gone then?
Your version of heaven is Extra
Strong Mints and Shingle Street,

Hot Toddies and furious walks
that follow a Scottish stream
to the edge of the world,
back to the arms of infinity —

wherever. Perhaps I will see your
face if I smash up a tea bag?

A bag within a bag you would say,
shrewd eyes flashing like an anorak.

Crumpet

The sky uses Google Images as her central
image and types *types of clouds* to learn more
about Cirrus Fibratus with their nice resonance.

Wikipedia is a man. Define Ezra Pound: *A visible mass
of condensed watery vapour floating in the atmosphere,
typically high above the general level of the ground.*

What is the etymology of etymology? Outer space burns
the sausages while looking for a soundclip on how
to pronounce *Abiogenesis* — if she says it wrong

at the reading everyone will know. Late Middle English:
from Old French *ethimologie*. Space sounds really clever —
a living organism arising naturally from non-living matter.

The moon writes a blog post about the death of her mother.
The tide likes it and turns toward a more empathetic
reading of the poet as a whole, waxing fat as a pregnant kite.

Embarrassed, the tide erases the clumsy kite image — the sand
blank and sophisticated once more. 'To flash the buttocks'

first recorded 1968, U.S. student slang, from moon (n.) 'buttocks'.

The audience will appreciate the humour, especially if they are present-day. A neutron star looks up synonyms for *relevance*, knocks one out for entire collapse — an intelligent entrant

that rotates for impending applause.

Troubadour

for Mark

No formula predicts the occurrence of
primes. Your random visits, barefoot toward
the ends of the earth became infinite —
the leaded pips of a loaded dice.

As you grew larger you became scarcer,
the distances got wider. We upset you
with the song *Winter*, careless the lines
about restoration, Stone Canyon — cold, cold.

You would not be pigeonholed. Gentle
crown of curls around the pinkest moon,
only as odd as the world beyond, refraction
caused by the crystals of a Magic Garden,

the silver-gold chains of a fierce intelligence.
Your wizard burden, yet. Duke of complex steps,
our Romeo & Juliet of the ringing woodlands,
renouncer of sable, vair, pact: Indivisible.